Ladybird,

Amanda Christie

Contents

OXFORD
UNIVERSITY PRESS

OXFORD
UNIVERSITY PRESS

Great Clarendon Street, Oxford, OX2 6DP

Oxford University Press is a department of the University of Oxford.
It furthers the University's objective of excellence in research, scholarship,
and education by publishing worldwide in

Oxford New York

Athens Auckland Bangkok Bogotá Buenos Aires Calcutta
Cape Town Chennai Dar es Salaam Delhi Florence Hong Kong Istanbul
Karachi Kuala Lumpur Madrid Melbourne Mexico City Mumbai
Nairobi Paris São Paulo Singapore Taipei Tokyo Toronto Warsaw
with associated companies in Berlin Ibadan

Oxford is a registered trade mark of Oxford University Press
in the UK and in certain other countries

© Oxford University Press 1999

The moral rights of the author have been asserted

Database right Oxford University Press (maker)

First published by Oxford University Press 1999
Reprinted 1999

A CIP record for this book is available from the British Library

ISBN 0 19 915751 0
Available in packs
Pack A Pack of Six (one of each book) ISBN 0 19 915756 1
Pack A Class Pack (six of each book) ISBN 0 19 915757 X

Printed in Hong Kong

Acknowledgements

The publisher would like to thank the following for permission
to reproduce photographs: Bruce Coleman/P. Kaya p 3, Bruce
Coleman/Andy Purcell p 9; FLPA/Peggy Heard p 7; Oxford Scientific
Films/ Avril Ramage pp 4, 5, Oxford Scientific Films p 10; Planet
Earth Pictures/Stephen P Hopkin p 6, Planet Earth Pictures p 8.

Illustration by Brett Breckon.

Front cover photograph by Planet Earth Pictures/Geoff du Feu.

With special thanks to Dr Michael Majerus, Department of
Genetics, Cambridge University.

Mating

Two ladybirds mated.

male
ladybird

female
ladybird

Eggs

The female
ladybird laid her
eggs on a leaf.

female
ladybird

eggs

The eggs hatched. Larvae came out.

larvae

FACT BOX
Insects' young are called "larvae".

Larvae and pupae

The larvae ate other insects.

larva

FACT BOX
One larvae is
called a "larva".

The larvae became pupae.

FACT BOX
Pupae have hard shells, and they do not eat.

Young ladybirds

A pupa split and a yellow ladybird came out.

8

The ladybird turned red and black spots formed.

FACT BOX
Some ladybirds stay yellow all their lives.

black spots

Mating

The ladybird found another ladybird to mate with.

male ladybird

female ladybird

The ladybird's lifecycle

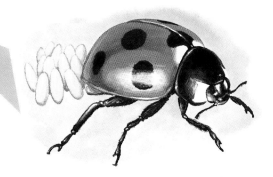

Day 1
mating
laying eggs

Day 11
eggs
hatching

Day 43
pupa
forms

Day 50
pupa splits

Day 52
ladybird
turns red

Index